INNER SIMPLICITY

Inner Simplicity

A LITTLE TREASURY

Elaine St. James

**Andrews McMeel
Publishing**

Kansas City

ISBN: 0-7407-0524-5

Library of Congress Catalog Card Number: 99-65539

The text of this book was previously published in Inner Simplicity *by Elaine St. James (© Hyperion 1995).*

Slow Down

The speed of life today permeates every area of our lives. For most of us, hurrying has become a habit. Even if you've simplified many of your daily routines, if you're still surrounded by fast-moving people and phones that never stop ringing, slowing down can take a major effort.

Start by thinking about how you can slow down your morning schedule. Getting up even half an hour earlier so you won't have to rush out the door will make a big difference in the pace of your entire day.

Take the time to sit down for your morning meal. Eat in a leisurely manner so you can feast on each bite. Eliminate the distractions of TV, radio, and the morning paper.

Make the preparation and consumption of food a conscious part of your inner quest, especially if you have lunch or dinner in fast-paced restaurants away from the peace and quiet you've established in your home.

Plan to leave home in plenty of time so you don't arrive at the office panting at the start of your workday. If possible, walk to work, or take the bus or some other form of public transportation so you won't have to compete in rush hour traffic. If you drive, make a point of staying within the posted speed limit. Learn to appreciate moving with purpose at a leisurely pace.

Make a concerted effort to examine all the areas of your life and figure out where you can slow down. If you've simplified your daily and weekly routines, you now have more time. Use some if it to reduce the over-all pace of your life so you can derive more pleasure from each thing you do throughout the day.

Slowing down will help you keep in touch with how you feel about what you're doing, and make it easier to connect with your inner self.

Spend Time Each Day in Nature

Many cultures throughout history have thought of nature as an integral and necessary part of their lives. Our society, for the most part, has lost contact with the restorative, healing, and inspirational power of the great outdoors.

Make spending time with nature an important part of your inner journey. If walking is included in your daily regimen, make sure that in addition to the physical and psychological benefits of being outdoors, you also connect on an inner level with the beauty of the sun and the sky and the earth.

Start each walk with an appreciation for the weather, no matter what it's doing. Make a point of delighting in the trees and birds and flowers and plant life on your route. Let the glories of nature energize your body, heal your psyche, and uplift your spirit.

If you don't exercise outdoors, at the very least make certain you spend a few moments each day cherishing and drawing energy from nature. Plan to leave your house five minutes early tomorrow morning. Before you get into your car or hop on the train, use those few minutes to notice the patterns of clouds in the sky or the dew on the grass. Or, take five minutes before you come into the house when you return from work, and simply acknowledge the closing of another day.

When weather permits, have your lunch outdoors on a park bench, or on the grass under the shade of a tree, and use the time to quietly commune with nature.

Before you go to bed at night, get into the habit of opening the front door and stepping outside for a few minutes. Encourage your spouse and your children to join you. You can all enjoy a deep breath of fresh air, and get lost in a silent, meditative look at the night sky.

If you live in the city and are surrounded

by tall buildings and concrete, make a point of taking advantage of nearby parks or public gardens. Be sure your schedule includes weekend trips to places where beauty has been allowed to flourish, and where you can use the power of nature to get in touch with who you really are.

Learn to Enjoy the Silence

In order to hear what's happening on an inner level, we have to cut back as much as possible on the external racket. Start becoming aware of the continuously high noise levels you are subjected to every day.

It often begins with the nerve-jangling clamor of the alarm clock, the buzz of an electric toothbrush, or the blast of a hair dryer. This is followed by the drone of the latest news report or the babble of morning talk shows. Then comes the revving of car engines, and the honking of horns in rush hour traffic.

Our days are often filled with the nine-to-five sounds of ringing telephones and office equipment, not to mention the countless interruptions of coworkers, customers, and bosses. Even if you work at home, there can be a constant din from which there is seldom any respite.

On weekends there's the roar of lawn mowers or leaf blowers. How can we possibly hear ourselves think?

Often we can't. We're stressed by all the noise in our day-to-day lives, frequently without even being aware of it. At the same time, we're so used to it that it's hard for us to imagine being without it.

As you begin to go within, you'll want to eliminate as much of the outer commotion as possible so you can hear your inner voice.

There may be some noises you won't have any control over, such as traffic or the festivities of neighbors. But you can start by creating as much quiet in your own space as possible.

Learn to wake up without an alarm: As you're about to fall asleep, simply visualize yourself waking up at whatever time you choose.

Try going without the TV or stereo for

periods of time. Leave your Walkman at home when you're walking or exercising, and keep your radio and tape player off, especially when you're driving. Bask in the silence, and use that time to be with the moment rather than letting those forms of entertainment distract you from your inner life.

Turn off your phone. Let your answering machine silently pick up messages, which you can listen to at your convenience.

Schedule a formal retreat at a nearby retreat center or arrange times of solitude at home so you can start tuning in to the joy of silence.

If you haven't been used to it, silence may seem strange at first, but you'll gradually come to treasure it. Eventually you'll find it indispensable for your inner search.

Create Your Own Sanctuary

It will be important for your inner pursuits to have a space you can call your own. It could be your own room, or even a small corner of a room. It will be somewhere you can go and not be disturbed.

This sanctuary will be where you'll pray, meditate, contemplate, do nothing, think, read, heal yourself, do your journal writing, and review your day. Do whatever you need to do to make it special and sacred.

Make sure you have a comfortable chair

and keep a supply of your favorite spiritual books nearby. Consider having a tape player and tapes of music you find uplifting. Have this be a place where you can go at any time to clear your energy, work out a problem, or to just sit quietly and *be*. Train your family not to interrupt you when you're there.

If you've never had the luxury of a place where you can go on a regular basis to get away from the daily routine of your life and be alone, don't waste another moment. This space will be essential for your spiritual growth.

Have a Weekend Retreat at Home

If you're working on establishing a level of inner simplicity, few things you can do will give you a better boost than a formal retreat. But if you're not quite ready to do that, or can't take the time right now, arranging your own retreat at home might be the next best thing.

Obviously, having a weekend retreat at home will be easier if you're single or if your spouse and children are either away for the weekend or are receptive to the idea of you taking some time on your own.

Set aside your normal weekend routine. Plan to start your quiet time by dinner on Friday evening and carry it through Sunday evening. Turn off the phone and let your answering machine or voice mail pick up messages for you. Tell your family and friends that you won't be available until Monday morning. Plan not to answer the door, or put a DO NOT DISTURB note on the door if necessary.

Do whatever you need to do to your space to make it conducive to quiet reflection. Air out the rooms; bring in fresh flowers; burn candles or incense or use essential oils. Have everything you might want at hand so you won't have to dash out into the world.

Keep the TV and radios off; put newspapers and magazines away. Take off your watch so you're not concerned with time. Wear loose-fitting, comfortable clothes. Avoid the type of food, drink, and other substances that will lower your energy.

Spend your time in silent contemplation. Meditate. Pray. Do yoga or gentle stretching. Do some deep breathing. Write in your journal. Watch sunsets and sunrises. Take a mini sun-bath to keep your mind and spirits elevated. Spend time in nature. Stroll in the early morning or evening, away from people and traffic. Sit quietly, not thinking, just being with the moment. Ask for guidance, and be open to whatever messages come to you.

Go to bed early and get up with the sun, or even earlier. If you rarely get to experience the joy of the birth of a new day, this is a good time to start.

Prepare your meals with love and awareness. Eat in silence without reading or any other distraction; make a point of savoring each bite.

Make a commitment to yourself not to worry or to engage in negative thinking during this time. If you feel lonely or frightened, write about your feelings in your journal.

This is a glorious opportunity to reconnect with your soul. Delight in it.

Have a Family Retreat

If your family is amenable, consider spending a silent meditative weekend retreat at home together. This can be a great way to strengthen the family bond.

If you haven't already established a pattern of regular times of solitude with your family, a retreat—even a quiet, contemplative afternoon together—would be a good way to start.

Enjoy Each Moment

One of the ultimate objectives of attaining inner simplicity is to learn to live happily in the present moment. Keep in mind that life is a continuous succession of present moments. Most of us spend an inordinate number of our moments regretting the past, fidgeting in the present, or worrying about the future. We miss a lot of life that way.

Worry and regret and being anxious are habits that keep us locked in old patterns. But these habits can be eliminated once we've become aware of them.

If you find such habits are getting in the way of being happy, think about what you can do to change them. It sounds simplistic, but you can get into the habit of enjoying your life.

One way to do that is to start taking responsibility for your life. If you're not happy in your present circumstances, you have no one but yourself to blame. Make whatever changes you need to make so you are happy.

By taking the time to become aware of the inner you, you'll automatically reach a level of enjoyment of your day-to-day life that you may not have experienced before. Making a conscious effort to enjoy each moment will make your inner quest that much easier.

Use the Events of the Day to Bring You Back

One of the benefits that comes from slowing down our lives is that it gives us the opportunity to get back in touch with who we really are and what we're doing here. It's quite liberating to make that connection, but often, because of the demands of our work schedule and the complexities of family and social obligations, we keep forgetting.

Get into the habit of using the events of your day to remind yourself of the inner realizations you are starting to get a sense of during your quiet times. You can use any circumstance or happening of the day to bring yourself back to the inner you.

When you wake up in the morning, remember. When you brush your teeth, remember. When the water boils for tea, remember.

When the phone rings, remember. When you are stopped at a stoplight, remember. When you sit down to a meal, remember. When you get upset, remember. When you have a headache, remember. When the kids are cranky, remember.

When you get into bed at night, remember. When you fall asleep, remember.

Learn to Receive

Get in the habit of receiving the benefits of the things you do. When you come in from your walk, take a few moments to absorb the contribution the exercise and the fresh air have made to your day and to your life.

When you finish a meal, sit quietly for a moment and be conscious of the nourishment the food brings to your body.

When someone pays you a compliment, instead of shrugging it off, accept it fully into your being—even revel in it. When you do something thoughtful for someone else, enjoy not only the pleasure they may derive from it, but the satisfaction it gives you to perform a good deed.

When you complete a project, take some time to acknowledge your accomplishment before you rush off to begin the next one.

So many extraordinary things happen to us throughout the day and throughout our lives. We often either ignore them, or make light of them as though they are unimportant. They are important. Take the time to notice them.

The little things take only a moment or two to acknowledge. All you have to do is stop for a couple of minutes and *receive.*

You'll know when you've taken it in completely, and when it's time to move on.

For the bigger things, like the achievement of a major goal, schedule whatever time you need to totally embrace the contribution you have made.

If you've simplified many areas of your life, you now have the time to assimilate into your being the synchronicities, the beauty, the love, the joys, and the work of your day. As they happen, let their beneficence pour over you and penetrate every fiber of your being.

In a very real sense, these daily events make you what you are. Savor them. Receive all the amity they have to offer.

Practice Detaching

When you find yourself in situations where your blood is boiling or your stomach is churning, try to get into the habit of stepping outside yourself and becoming the observer.

This is easier to do in the heat of the moment if you've practiced it before the battle gets started.

Whenever you find yourself going through a particularly difficult time, make a point of taking five or ten minutes at the end of the day to practice detaching.

Perhaps you've had an argument with a coworker, or a disagreement with your spouse. As soon as you have the opportunity, sit quietly and imagine being back in that scene.

See in your mind's eye the inner you stepping away from the fracas and simply observing what's going on. Run through the entire altercation in your mind with the inner you not being part of it, simply watching from the sidelines.

If you practice this consistently, not only will you find that it relieves some of the tension of the current problem you're dealing with, but it will become an automatic response you can fall into when you find yourself in the fray again.

Detaching releases tension, diffuses the negative energy, and helps you to see the insignificance of this event in the whole scheme of things. It also gives you a chance to see what lessons you might need to learn from this encounter.

Choose to Ignore an Insult

There is a Chinese proverb that says it is better to ignore an insult than to respond to one. There is such wisdom here.

Think of the troubles you could avoid and the stress you could eliminate if you made the decision to ignore a slight offense or a minor defamation or an unintentional snub—or even an intentional one. Our reaction to the situations of our lives are elective, and *we* get to do the electing.

The next time someone is rude to you,

fail to notice it. It's a choice. Or choose to be tolerant or gracious or forgiving.

This is not to say you should let everyone walk all over you. But you may well find as you continue along your path that it's much more exhilarating to keep your head clear for contemplating the big picture.

Ignoring an insult is a foolproof way to keep from getting bogged down in someone else's negative energy, or even in your own.

Use Affirmations

An affirmation is a mental or verbal declaration to yourself and to the universe about how you want your life to be. Words and thoughts are powerful things. Your life as it is right now is in large part a physical manifestation of all your past thoughts, both positive and negative.

Positive affirmations are an effective way to clear the negativity out of our minds and our lives, and to propel us along in our efforts to make our lives exactly the way we want them.

Take some time in the next few days to come up with a personal statement that expresses the thing or things you most want in your life right now, such as peace, tranquility, simplicity, wisdom, enlightenment, spiritual growth, whatever.

Make your affirmation a positive statement that declares to yourself and to the universe that you have this thing or quality in your life right now, such as "I live a simple, peaceful life."

It doesn't matter if the statements you affirm are not true yet. Repetition of an affirmation, combined with belief and imagination, enhances the ability of your subconscious mind to bring about the reality you affirm.

You can use a journal to record these affirmations for your daily use. Get into the habit of actively thinking about and repeating selected ones to yourself throughout the day. Keep a rubber band around your wrist or use Post-it notes as a reminder until the habit of working with your affirmations for your inner growth is firmly established.

Then be prepared to change and adapt your affirmations as your life changes and you gradually become the person you affirm yourself to be.

Use Visualizations

In addition to verbally affirming the inner qualities you want to develop, you can create a clear mental image that projects what you want your life to look like. This focuses your attention on that outcome and helps bring it into your life.

Numerous studies have shown how effective visualization can be for healing and personal growth, and in sports and physical achievements. Like affirmations, visualizations are potent tools for your spiritual journey.

Spend some quiet time in your sanctuary thinking about how you would look and feel if you had the inner qualities of love, compassion, gratitude, understanding, patience, and joy.

Pick one trait, such as compassion, and step into it each morning as part of your daily routine. Make this a habit. In your mind's eye, actually *see* yourself having this quality. Imagine how you would look and how you would feel if you had compassion. Check with yourself throughout the day to make sure this feeling of compassion is still with you. Do this until you've absorbed this quality. Then move on to the next one.

We're continually bombarded with negative messages that can easily deflect us from our search for inner peace. Developing the ability to counteract that negativity with positive mental images will go a long way toward keeping you on track.

Review Your Day

Take a few minutes each evening just before bedtime to review your day. Go to your sanctuary, and start by sitting quietly for a few moments to let the vibes from the day settle down. Take a couple of long, slow, deep breaths, and consciously relax your body. Have the intention of getting rid of any worries or concerns. If you're tuned in, you can actually feel any negative energy slowly dissipate.

Then do a quick review of your day, and take particular notice of any issue you may want to deal with. Do what you can to bring a level of understanding to this, then release it. Sometimes, just letting go of a dilemma brings a clarity that will help you address it later from a more enlightened point of view.

You can sit there for a few blissful moments and be grateful for your day. You can prepare for your dream explorations. If you're developing any affirmations or new practices you want to incorporate into your life—or getting rid of any bad habits—keep your journal handy to chart your progress.

These few moments at the end of the day will give you a chance to slow down, unwind, enjoy the silence, and tap into any messages from your inner self that might assist you as you go along. Not only will it help you stay on course for the things you want to accomplish at an inner level, but clearing away any mental, emotional, or psychic clutter will make it easier for you to get a good night's sleep.

When you spend time reviewing your life on a daily basis, you'll see that each day presents an opportunity to live your life exactly the way you want to. Imagine yourself moving into the best you can be, and then living each subsequent day from that perspective. With time, you'll get better and better at doing this.

Be Patient

One of the exciting things about the times in which we live is that we can do almost anything we want to do. Our advancing technology makes it possible for us to have and do things that previous generations never dreamed of. We've gotten used to the instant gratification of our wants and desires. This makes being patient more challenging than it might be otherwise.

As we begin to go within and start to address the big issues, as we learn to love and to forgive, as we overcome our fears and learn to say no to the distractions, it becomes easier to create happier, more ful-filling lives.

But there are still hurdles to overcome. The technology is not yet available that would make it possible for us to conquer our demons overnight. The process of growth in any endeavor can often seem like one step forward and two steps back-ward.

Sometimes you may be disconcerted when you look at your list of things you've wanted to accomplish. Six months ago you may have checked forgiveness off your list, only to find now that it's back in your life again as an issue you have to deal with. It may feel as though you have to start all over. But as you begin to examine it, you'll see how much the work you've previously done has helped.

Use a journal to help you keep track of your progress, and learn to be patient with yourself. Enjoy the process of inner growth for what it is—an ongoing opportunity to become the best you can become at all levels of your life.

Don't push the river. Just let it flow.

Practice Dying

Years ago a teacher I studied with guided us through a meditation in which we confronted our own death. Coming, as many of us have, from a background in which the actuality of death was seldom discussed, much less thought about, I found this somewhat startling at first. But after I'd gone through the exercise a number of times, I began to appreciate the benefits it offered. I started to see death as simply a natural process, and nothing to be afraid of.

Some years later I found myself in the

middle of a hurricane with six other people in a very small boat on a very large ocean. I lived for forty-eight hours in the certain belief that we wouldn't survive. When I thought about it later, I was surprised at how calm I felt. It seemed as though I'd done this many times before—which of course I had, through the practice of the dying meditation.

Many cultures throughout history have practiced dying as a ritual. It is a way to confront the fear of death in order to loosen its hold on us. Once you get into it, it can be quite liberating.

So practice dying. Do this as a meditation, and as an exercise in personal growth.

Set aside some time in the next week to

imagine your own death. Lie down. Close your eyes. Imagine that you are dying. Where are your friends and family? What do you feel? What are they feeling? Is there anyone you have unfinished business with whom you need to talk to? What would you say to the people you would leave behind?

Then imagine that you are dead. Gone. The End.

This can be terrifying. Even if you envision that you're surrounded by people you love and who love you, there comes a point when you have to take that last step seemingly alone. Even though it's only an exercise, go with it. Experience that terror. It'll free you.

After you've gone through your first

imaginary encounter with your own death, spend some time thinking about other ways you might die: alone in your car on a deserted stretch of highway, or in an airplane crash with hundreds of other people. Run through all kinds of possibilities.

Engaging in the practice of dying, if done with sincerity and as an inquiry into the phenomenon of death, will liberate you from any fear of death you might have, and free you from many other fears as well.

Just think how you could live your life with full abandon if your fear of death were no longer there to hold you back.

Harbor No Thought
That Will Burn

Letting go of negative thinking might seem to be a never-ending battle. Our thoughts define our universe, and if we've spent years operating out of negative thought patterns, sometimes seemingly successfully, there can be a part of us that doesn't want to give it up.

Perhaps you know the type of thinking I'm referring to: the huffing and puffing and steaming and fuming over insignificant inanities that never in a lifetime are worth the emotion spent on them. It's not difficult to figure out the kinds of thoughts that are keeping you from having peace of mind, and from moving on to a higher level of being.

You can glom on to every tool in your arsenal to overcome negative thinking. Use affirmations and visualizations. Connect with nature. Do some deep breathing. Develop self-discipline. Use your willpower. Keep your energy up. Chant. Meditate. Pray.

It may take a major effort, but it will be vital for your progress on your inner path to become aware of the self-defeating mental grooves you sometimes function in, and to make the decision to change them.

Stop Worrying

Worry is a habit. Like any other habit, it can be broken once we become aware of it. But worry is sometimes so subtle and so insidious—and so pervasive in our society—that we can worry for years and not even be aware of it.

I learned this lesson a few years back when I had completed a major promotional project for a company I worked for. After months of long, hard, demanding hours and many sleepless nights when I would lie awake worrying if everything would be all right, the deadline was met and the project was finally completed. It was out of my hands; there was not a single thing more I could possibly do about it.

One night a few weeks later, before I had had a chance to start another project, I realized I was still waking in the middle of the night and lying there worrying—even though there was nothing at all to worry about.

As I lay there, I had one of those lightbulb experiences we all have from time to time. I saw in a flash that I'd been moving through life from one worry to the next. I examined each of the circumstances as I could remember them, and it became clear that not only had there never been anything to worry about, but worrying had never served any useful function. It was simply a bad habit that wasted my energy and kept me from experiencing the joy of the moment. It also kept me from getting any real sense of accomplishment from my work.

Do whatever you need to do to eliminate worry. A worry-free life will go a long way toward helping you achieve inner peace.

Stop Judging Others

One of the problems that comes from being raised in a patriotic and chauvinistic culture like ours is that we are bred from birth to believe in our own superiority.

It's not only patriotism that instills this conviction. Our religions, our ethnic backgrounds, our educational and cultural training, and the media we are exposed to all teach us, sometimes inadvertently, that we're supposed to be better than the next guy.

Often we go through life believing it's

natural to look down on someone else because of the way they dress, where they live, the work they do, the amount of money they have in the bank, and whether or not they use deodorant soap.

This pervades every area of our lives. We are bombarded daily with hundreds of judgments, many of which we're not even consciously aware of.

When we start to glimpse the possibility that we're here for reasons other than owning a house on two acres and a four-wheel drive vehicle, we get the opportunity to take a look at our judgments and to see how they get in the way of our inner growth.

Once you start to understand that you're here for some other purpose, then you have to make the connection that we're all here for some other purpose, even if we don't all realize it, and even if we don't know what that purpose is yet.

At some point we begin to get the picture that we're all in this together, and that we're each doing the best we can with what we've got. It's not our place to judge where someone else is on their path.

The process of learning to suspend our judgment about other people and situations can be a particularly arduous one because we have so much training to overcome. But, as with other habit patterns, overcoming it starts with the awareness of how judgmental we are in every area of our lives.

Once we begin to see how often we subtly dismiss others because they don't live up to our standards, we can slowly start to let go of our judgments and get back to trying to figure out what we came here to do. And then get on with it.

Take Time to Think

One of the frequent comments I hear from people is, "It's so obvious what I need to do to simplify my life. I could have figured out how to do it myself if I'd just *thought* about it."

They're absolutely right. The changes we need to make to our lives are the obvious ones. But we're often too busy to stop and *think* about what we need to do to bring them about. We've been so caught up in the stress and the pressures and the demands of our days that we've gotten out of the habit of *thinking*.

As you set out and continue along your path of inner simplicity, be sure to set aside time to think on a regular, even daily, basis. Get in the habit of spending a few minutes in the morning before you start your day thinking about how you want to be in your work and in your interactions with the people you come into contact with.

Then, at the end of the day, take a few minutes to think about how you did in relation to how you wanted to do.

Think about the things that may have kept you from enjoying your day, or from living it the way you'd like to. Then think about how you might do things differently tomorrow.

In addition to the daily evaluations, we need to set aside larger blocks of time to think about the big picture. Use some of your regularly scheduled times of solitude to really *think* about your inner life and your outer life, where you want to go with each, and what kinds of things you can do to get there.

Set aside time for weekend or longer retreats, and use the time to question your long-accepted assumptions or beliefs. There are few things as liberating as coming up with your own solutions to your own issues.

All the information we need to know about our lives and how to live them is available to us. Thinking is one of the tools we can use to tap into that information.

Get Rid of Your Anger

Every morning for the next week, before
you start your day, go to your bedroom,
close the door, and pile all your pillows in the
center at the head of the bed. Kneel on the
bed with the pillows in front of you. Bow
gently to your inner self and to the universe.
Then start beating the living daylights out of
the pillows.

Do this as a spiritual exercise. Use either
your fists, another pillow, or a plastic baseball
bat. Do it for five to ten minutes, or longer if
that feels appropriate.

When the time is up, fall into a heap on the bed and breathe deeply until you catch your breath. When you've come back to your center, get up, kneel on the bed as before, and bow again to yourself and the universe. Then go about your day.

You won't believe the feeling of lightness you'll have after doing this. There are so many messages waiting to come to us, they can't easily move through the negativity of anger and the bad feelings we frequently carry with us.

Get in touch with how you deal with anger. Do you clam up? Do you harbor burning thoughts? Do you take your anger out on others? Whenever you find your-

self reacting in these or any other counter-
productive ways of denying anger, go to
the pillows and beat the living daylights out
of them for at least five minutes, or as long
as it takes. Teach your kids to do this, too.

You may have to replace your pillows
frequently. But that's preferable to having
to replace your stomach lining, or a heart
valve.

Cry a Lot

Crying is an effective way to clear out the stuff that gets in the way of our inner growth.

It's possible you need to cry and you're not aware of it. Or maybe you spend much of your time on the brink of tears.

In either case, arrange your schedule so you can cry every morning for the next week or however long is necessary. Do this as a spiritual exercise and be open to the benefits it will bring to your life.

Allow thirty minutes for the crying; longer if possible. You'll need at least that much time to get the floodgates open. If you get a good cry going, don't stop just because the time is up. Cry to the end of the cry.

You may need to fake it to begin with. The more drama you can put into it to start with, the better. You may go for several days with only fake tears. That's all right. Eventually real tears will come. Keep at it until they do.

We've been told for so long that it's not okay to cry. But it *is* okay. In fact, it's desirable. More than that, it's vital. The energy we've been using to hold back the tears is getting in the way of being who we truly are. Let that energy go, and cry. It'll free you.

Laugh a Lot

Every day for the next week, spend five or ten minutes laughing, first thing in the morning. Do this in your sanctuary, at your kitchen table, or wherever works for you. This may not be easy. We aren't encouraged to laugh a lot in this culture. But if you do this, you'll be amazed at the insight it will give you.

As with the crying, you may have to start by faking it. You may have to fake it all the way through. That's okay. Pretend you're an actor, laughing for a part. It's easier if you stand, or sit on the edge of a chair. After the first few times, your stomach muscles will ache a bit. It's nothing to worry about. Keep at it.

When you're finished laughing, sit quietly and receive. Let your body and your psyche and your soul absorb the benefits. Then start your day.

It's a lot of fun to do this with someone else who is amenable, but don't let the absence of an available person keep you from laughing. It's just as beneficial to do it on your own.

When the week is up, or possibly even sooner, you'll see that it's possible for you to laugh at anything; that laughter is a choice.

As you move along in your quest, and as you encounter seemingly difficult situations, don't forget to laugh. It will change your life.

Also, make a point of spending time with people who make you laugh. Rent funny videos. Read funny books. Laughing is so good for the soul.

Create Joy in Your Life

A while back I took a stroll down to the beach at sunset. It was one of those spectacular displays that casts a rosy glow, seemingly over the entire creation. There were a few wisps of white clouds in the sky, and as the sun sank lower on the horizon, the clouds became tinged with pink. Within a few moments, they had changed color entirely as they totally absorbed the brilliant hue of the sun. Venus began to be visible in the western sky.

I looked to the east, and saw the nearly

full moon rising huge and golden. I watched as the sky changed from one glorious shade to another. I was so enthralled with this exquisite display that I felt nearly full to overflowing with what I can only call unbounded joy.

The next day I found myself starting to succumb to a difficult moment in my work. Perhaps because this irksome note was in such contrast to the continued delight I had been feeling from the previous evening, and because that enjoyment had been so complete, I immediately recalled that sunset. Instantly the difficulty was overshadowed by the re-creation of the joy I'd experienced the night before. It wasn't that I was living in the past, but that by an act of will I was able to bring that joy to the present.

As the days and weeks passed, I found I was able to tap into that joy again and again, and to absorb it into the present moment. Even now, months later, I'm still getting mileage from that sunset.

We all have these moments in our lives. They are available to us in one degree or another every single day. We can find them in the smile of someone we love, or in the smile of someone we don't even know. We can find them in the hug of a child, in the presence of a friend, or the touch of a lover.

Think about the times in your life when you've been overcome with joy. It's in those moments that you're in love with yourself and everyone else. It's in those moments you believe you can conquer the world. It's in those moments that you dare to imagine how you want your life to be.

It's from that imagination and that belief and that love that we can and do create our lives.

Think about the things that bring you joy, then make a point of connecting with as many of them as possible, as often as possible.